I0469655

Writing With Other People's Content

Profitable Strategies For Using Private Label Rights Materials In Your Business Revealed

Thom Lancaster
&
Garry Sayer

The content for this book is sourced mainly from training seminars carried out by Thom Lancaster, and is used under license.

Dedicated to quality writers everywhere.

Writing With Other People's Content

Profitable Strategies For Using Private Label Rights Materials In Your Business Revealed

Table of Contents

About The Author

Thom Lancaster is a UK based Internet Marketer. He has a particular interest in product creation.

To find out more about Thom, visit ThomLancaster.com.

Garry Sayer is a part time Internet Marketer who also runs his own successful software distribution business.

Garry Sayer offers exclusive PLR packages with Thom Lancaster at 10BuckPLR.com.

Foreward

Buying PLR, or Private Label Rights, is the fastest way to having your own ready to sell product. Marketers have recognized this huge demand and capitalized on it. Unfortunately some use it as an opportunity to flood the market with inferior PLR. Now more than ever you need to be savvy with the PLR you buy and how you repurpose it. Thom Lancaster is an absolute genius with PLR and inside this book he reveals the same strategies that have generated him lots of cold hard cash.

The first problem face is judging the quality of the PLR. How can you identify the good PLR from the bad? It's difficult. Sometimes I've been drawn in by the professionally designed graphics only to be instantly disappointed the moment I downloaded and opened the product. Other times I've purchased PLR that visually doesn't look that great but the content's incredible. Thom shares with you exactly how to identify good PLR from the shoddy stuff that's out there. This information is priceless and will save you a ton of time and money!

The second problem many people face is what to do with PLR once they get it. Many will simply upload it to their hosting server as it comes. This will generate you some sales but there's so much more you can do with PLR. Other people own the same PLR license and product as you so you need to separate yourself from them. Thom really knows his stuff on this subject and the insight you'll receive from this book will help you get extra profit from your PLR. I frequently buy and repurpose PLR yet even I learned many helpful tips and tricks in this book.

10BuckPLR.com

The demand for high-quality PLR products is almost insatiable but unfortunately the market is flooded with inferior quality PLR. My business partner Thom Lancaster and I try and deliver the only the best with 10buckplr.com.

Garry Sayer
10BuckPLR.com

Chapter 1 – Introduction

Welcome to **Writing With Other People's Content**. It's a slightly cheeky name for a guide about how you can use Private Label Rights content as either a writer or a business, to save yourself a lot of time, or to produce a much better finished product.

Before I start this chapter, I want to make one thing totally clear. In this book I'm not advocating stealing content. I'm only suggesting you use the hard work of other people that has led to the creation of high quality content in a totally legal and ethical way.

That's the whole beauty of Private Label Rights content and why it has beend developed. It's content that people are wanting you to reuse, and which they are expecting you to reuse.

Whether you use PLR (that's the short way of referring to Private Label Rights content) online or offline, it can make you a lot of money. It can also be used to increase your reputation and name value. After all, the more products (of quality) you have your name on, the more important you'll be perceived as being to a wider audience.

Do take your time to read this book thoroughly, and be willing to duck in and out of the content as it most appeals to be you.

Most importantly, put the ideas you read into practice. That's where the real value of PLR lies. There's nothing to be gained by buying PLR content and having it sat on your bookshelf (or your virtual bookshelf, as you may consider your hard drive).

Using the PLR is the real secret!

10BuckPLR.com

Chapter 2 – Overview Of The Book

I've split this book into the four main areas which I think will really help you to understand and use PLR in the best manner.

First of all, in Chapter 3, I want to make sure you understand what private label rights content is. A lot of people get the definitions wrong, and that can be a disaster, especially as you're using other people's content to represent yourself. It's all based around a set of rights which tell you how you can use the PLR.

In Chapter 4, I'm going to show you how you can identify good PLR, because the big difference between Private Label Rights content you can make money from, and PLR content that's just no great use to you. It really is worthwhile buying better quality content to repurpose.

In Chapter 5, I'm just going to share with you how you can make this PLR unique. This gives you a huge advantage when selling in the marketplace. It's when you really do seem to be writing with other people's content.

I want to finish the training section of the book with some really juicy tips that can make you a lot of money if you apply them. These will help you to get extra profit from PLR content. Once you have a good understanding of PLR, I recommend you focus on Chapter 6 in depth.

Finally, in Chapter 7, I'm going to end with some motivating words and advice. I want to leave you ready to profit from all the new PLR tricks you've discovered at the end of this valuable training resource.

10BuckPLR.com

Chapter 3 – Understanding PLR

It's really important to start your PLR training with a thorough understanding of what PLR means and how you can legally reuse it.

Let's start with the basics. PLR stands for Private Label Rights. And this is a type of content which you can purchase the rights to use as if it was material you had personally written. In many ways, it's better than employing a ghostwriter, as this PLR will be sold to multiple people. Because of that, you're getting something which has been little seen, but at a fraction of the price of hiring someone to write it for you from scratch.

You can edit the PLR, and make it into your own product. Once it has been edited, no one need ever know that the source of this product wasn't directly out of your own brain.

You're getting a solution where the research is done for you, which is a huge time saver. You've got a product almost ready to go, out of the box. So if you go ahead and you buy an eBook for instance, which comes with private label rights.

You can then just change the eBook around, and sell it as if you've written it yourself. And that's a huge time saver. You might think it might take a good person twenty hours to make a product. You can the same thing in just an hour or two by strategically using content that you've purchased those private label lights to.

Now when you do get your PLR eBook, or whatever the package may be. It's very important to check the right statement contained within it, because exactly what you're allowed to do with each product will vary. For instance, some products will allow you to claim copyright, and others will not. Some products will allow you to sell the item that you just purchased for an extremely low price on some auction sites. Others may not.

This rights statement will set out exactly what you should be expecting from this package. And if you should look at this, you can make an intelligent decision about whether this PLR content is for you. One thing you should always look at in a rights statement is whether the PLR comes with any type of transferrable resell rights.

As a buyer of PLR, you will always be allowed to sell the product you've created. However, some people like to also allow their customers to sell this product too. The reasoning is, they can sell this product for more money as the rights make it a commodity which is in greater demand.

To do that, you need to have master resell rights? Which means, you can then allow other people also to sell the finished product.

Sometimes the PLR rights statements will allow you to transfer the Private Label Rights itself. This means that you can pass on the Word document, either in an edited format, or just exactly how you purchased it.

In other cases, the rights may mean that buyers can sell only the compiled version of the document, so you'd usually take a PLR document and convert it to a pdf.

Either of these are quite acceptable, depending on the right statement which comes with the package. If a product has resell rights, it will give you more options, if you can transfer them, which is commonly known as master resell rights. Alternatively, the product may just come allowing you to transfer personal rights to your customer. That can be high valued PLR in its on right.

Hopefully this chapter has given you enough of an overview about what PLR content is, so you know how you can take out an eBook, or what may be a set of articles, what may be a video product, or what may be a software product.

There's all sorts of private label rights content out there. Make sure you check the rights statement carefully so you know exactly what you can do with it. That has a major effect on how you profit from PLR.

10BuckPLR.com

Chapter 4 – Identifying Top Quality PLR

Very simply, when you're writing with other people's content, you only want to put your name on a product which oozes quality. Now, it can be possible to take a product which isn't brilliant and to polish it up; that's what the PLR rights allow you to do. But, it's definitely better to start off with high quality material that does not require this level of changes.

Before you go out and buy PLR, you need to make an intelligent decision about what PLR is worth purchasing. Are you going to be able to identify good PLR? And I write this with a slight warning, because not all PLR content is of the same standard.

Just imagine if you could go out and buy an eBook purely for your own personal use. Some eBooks will be better than others. It's exactly the same as purchasing a PLR eBook. And some of them will not be well written. And you need to always be looking for content that's being written to a high standard.

You want it to have been produced by a native English speaker, because your customers, when they buy the version of the product that you can use from the PLR, will much prefer to have a high quality product produced by a native English speaker.

And you want it to read like one continuous book. Occasionally, you come across a PLR report which looks as if it has been written by a whole host of different people, and then all the individual elements have just been plastered together to form an in-cohesive whole. That's bad PLR. You need to be looking for that. And if you can see samples of PLR before you start, or samples of the compiled version, then that's a good starting point. But perhaps more importantly, you need the PLR to have a limited distribution. For instance, one hundred copies is a good number.

What that means is there won't be too many people who you're competing with to sell the same content. And that's a huge advantage to you as a marketer, as you try and position yourself in the marketplace, with this PLR content. So look for PLR, which is only distributed to a very small number, or a limited number of people. Now ideally your PLR is going to be ready to go. And what that means is you can purely purchase a package, and you can take it, you can immediately put it up on your website, possibly without making any changes at all, and it's ready for you to make sales from it straightaway.

What do we mean by ready to go here? It's simple. You get the files for a complete sales process. There's no messing about, nothing you need to do to it. It's in such a good state, you'd be happy to sell it as is, without having to go through, proofread it, and correct it. Perhaps more importantly, it comes with some graphics to help support it, maybe only some very limited graphics, because graphics doesn't make a very huge difference to sales. But just something simple like an eCover, can make the difference when you're selling online.

As well as that, a ready to go product should comes with sales copy to help you to sell it. What this means, is you have a sales letter advertising the product, which is ready prepared for you, because it's going to be quite a big job to write a sales copy, particularly if you're not experienced at it. Because there are certain advertising commercial techniques which help products to sell and it's exactly the same with content that's based on PLR. If you get a good sales copy, then you're ready to go.

One final thing I think you should look at when identifying good PLR, is the topic of the PLR.

If you want to sell, you want topics which are hot in the marketplace. For instance, in the internet marketing niche, which I'm sure many people who are listening to this audio tutorial, will be interested in, you'd be looking for items which are very popular at the moment.

For instance, I'll give you an example. Fiverr, the outsourcing site for low cost outsourcing, is incredibly hot right now. Everybody wants to get into that site, either to sell their services for five dollars a time, or to get things for them by paying out five dollars a time.

That's the kind of hot niche you should be looking for, if you want to do well from PLR content in the internet marketing niche. So make sure you're ready to identify good PLR, and you buy PLR with limited distribution, which you know has been written to high standard on a popular topic, and is ready to go. You can profit well from the PLR if you follow those simple steps.

Chapter 5 – Separating Your PLR Product From The Pack

In this chapter, I want to tell you a little bit about how you can make the PLR content unique. This is important. It will give you an extra selling point in the marketplace and reduce your competition, because your PLR will look different to the same product being sold by other marketers. I hope you can understand why making your PLR product unique is incredibly powerful.

Because if you can make your PLR unique, but only spend a small amount of time on it, that's so you can get all this done in sixty minutes or less, then you've got a huge advantage. So how do we go about these simple steps? Well I'm going to give you one huge tip here. And you need to do this every single product without fail. It will take you about thirty seconds per product or less. And that's to come up with a new name for the product. Because that's one step that many of your competitors will just miss out.

By giving the product a new name, you immediately have your PLR set up in a way that other customers who are searching for that, won't find the same product on the internet being sold by anyone else.

Let's have a look at the example again that we started in Chapter 4. If we're working on a product on Fiverr, then you just give it a different name. You make sure you keep Fiverr in the title. So, Fiverr Instant Profit Secrets can be one name. What other kinds of names could you go for? Make Money from Fiverr Today. That would be pretty much, say it again, same kind of thing, but appealing to a different audience. Just come up with a new name to go with that.

When you change the name, all you have to do is change inside the source file. Change it in the source copy that comes with it. If there are any graphics, then and just update that on the graphics, very simple to change the text on graphics.

That will give you a unique PLR product. You've now invented a unique product to sell, which people won't even know is based on private label rights content. What else can you do to make it unique? You can spend just a little bit more time on changing things around.

For instance, by rewriting the sales copy, and you can definitely do this in an hour, all you want to do is to take the existing copy as a base, and come up with some new elements to it. Change it around a bit. Change some words here or there. Perhaps use a different headline to replace the existing one. Again, this gives you a bit more uniqueness. And you can test out headlines you think might work out better for your particular audience, because only you know how your customer base you've already established work.

Then make an angle you know about, which you can capitalize on and work into the sales copy. For instance, if you have a list aimed purely at mums who want to make money online, then perhaps you can work that angle into your sales copy, for a more general product. So, How Mums can Make Money by Using Fiverr.

That's only a simple change to the copy. But if you can bring in some examples about other mums you've found on Fiverr already, then you've got a perfect solution there. So you can rewrite the sales copy.

If you want to make your product look completely different, you could produce an entirely new set of graphics to go with it. Now you don't have to do this yourself. You could outsource this. For instance, you could go to Fiverr, which you just mentioned as a site, and paste them on five dollars to come up with a new eCover. So that's a very small investment that will give you something that looks completely different. And some buyers do look at the graphics, and people who have a visual brain will recognize if they've seen that design before or not. Now that may be a minor point.

There's a good chance if they've come directly through your sales funnel that the buyers will not know about this. But it's definitely something worth bearing in mind. And if you want to spend just a little bit more time and to convert PLR eBook into a high ticket product, then the best thing you can do is to convert that product into a video. I'm going to give you a simple process to complete this. All you need is PowerPoint. If you don't have PowerPoint, you can use the OpenOffice alternative, which has some presentation software built in, and put together some simple slides which cover the items in the table of contents, from the video. Sorry, from the report.

If your report has ten chapters, you could come up with ten slides. On each slide, you just need five or six bullet points which cover the main elements of that chapter, and simple record a screen capture video of yourself talking through the different slides. If you find it easier, you can even print out a copy of the eBook, and read that with the slides on the screen. Or you can view the eBook on a second monitor if you're fortunate enough to have two monitors, which is a power productivity tip, which is great when you're working with PLR.

That should give you some ideas about how to make your PLR unique, without spending a lot of time, and to give you an extra advantage in the market, just by looking at renaming the product. That's so crucial. Never miss that step. You can change the sales copy. You can ask somebody to produce new graphics for you, or produce them yourself if you're graphically talented, or convert the product to video, which can be great for taking a seven dollar product, and selling it at twenty seven dollars, because of the high perceived value that video has.

10BuckPLR.com

Chapter 6 – Extra Profit From PLR

Once you've mastered the basics of PLR, it's really important to work out how you can get the highest financial return from it. This is when writing with other people's content can really help you.

The techniques I'm exposing to you in this chapter are also powerful. They don't need to take you much time to set up, but can bring you in the extra income for years to come. And this is about thinking smartly when you're working with this PLR content.

The very first thing to do is take the report, which will probably come in the form of a Microsoft Word document, to be able to edit it in Word or OpenOffice, and add affiliate links into that report for other products for which you can receive a commission if a sale is made.

For instance, if the report talks about the need for hosting service, then you could sign up as an affiliate for hosting service, and add you link to the report, so people click through that, and they take a posting based on the offer, and make some money from it. You can also add links to any of the products you've products. So if you've got a whole product line of different products which you've put together from PLR, then why not add links to all of those, because you make extra sales immediately from those products, purely by mentioning them on a resources page, or sprinkling them into the text of your new product.

This means that affiliate links and links to other offers are particularly important.

Another thing you can do is to bundle PLR products together, as is particularly useful when the products have been out for a while, to go back and to look at some of your older products, and see if you can make a bundle offer. For instance, offer three of them for the price of two, because that can be a powerful technique, to bundle PLR together. Now I suggest you don't do this with fresh on the market products, that you take full advantage of these, and make money from these products, especially if they're a hot topic, as we mentioned earlier.

But, if they've been out for a while, then you can stand to look at bundling, because there's no reason why you shouldn't make full use of any product that you've created. So, always consider bundling the PLR together.

How else can you profit from PLR? You can add extra components to a simple eBook, to improve it. For instance, one component you can put together, which doesn't take you very long, is a worksheet. Think of some questions that somebody will have, or some way of testing that they understand the information presented in the report, and put together a simple worksheet, which may only be one page or two pages long with some questions, the kind of things they have to ask themselves.

So for instance, if you're doing a Fiverr product, we'll go back to the same example we've been using throughout this book. Then what kind of worksheet could you have? You could ask people, you can say, what type of skills do you have? What kind of services do you think you could offer on Fiverr? You could even ask some questions like, do you think there's a good market for these services on Fiverr? How many competitors are there? And just a few simple steps which they can take, and you'll have a service for them that's ready to go.

Any extra components you can add, such as worksheets, are particularly useful to differential your PLR from others on the market. And you'll get extra profit, because you'll make more sales for that small amount of effort required to put those extra components together.

I have one more way to share with you that can help you make extra profit from PLR. That's by selling an audio version, as well as a printed eBook version. All you have to do to produce an audio version, is get a microphone and record yourself reading the eBook.

Provided you've got a pretty clear voice that goes down very well because people are happy to pay for an audio version, even if they've already got the printed version. That's because an audio version has many advantages. Your customer could listen to the audio when they're not in front of the computer, when they're driving, when they're working around the house, when they're out in the garden, because nearly everybody nowadays has got an mp3 player, or an iPod, to listen to it. Or, if nothing else, they can listen on a mobile phone which will play back these recordings.

You can offer this as an up sell service where people buy the eBook, and then get the option of paying a small extra fee to get the audio version as well. By spending that time recording it, and the audio version needs only take real time to create, then you have a powerful extra profit tool.

The best thing to do is to put all these ideas together, if you get any extra profit from your PLR, you add affiliate links strategically to the document. You add extra components such as worksheets, and put these together. You look at bundling multiple products when they're at the end of their shelf life, and you sell an audio version as well, then you've immediately got a lot of extra profit from a product, from a set of activities which won't take you long to put together.

And none of these aspects need to take you very long to put together.

10BuckPLR.com

Chapter 7 – Your PLR Action Plan

Thanks for reading **Writing With Other People's Content**. I want to end this book with some motivating advice for you.

The main thing is that you need to apply all the techniques you've discovered in this book. They are there to help you to profit from PLR. They are all real techniques and they all work in practice. There's no hiding behind theory.

10BuckPLR.com

Go out and purchase a high quality PLR product to use. I recommend you start off at 10BuckPLR.com. It's a site which combines a low cost entry point to PLR with high quality exclusive content with limited distributed. All the topics we discussed in Chapter 4 which help you to work with better PLR.

The 10 Buck PLR has been written by native English speakers, and it's been put together on hot topics in internet marketing that you know sell, because you are going to see other people who are doing it. You can get these products that are ready to go.

All you need to do is to upload them to your site. They come complete with sales copies for making profit very quickly. I'd suggest you just rename the products, and you're ready to go. If you're feeling great, you can do more work. But when you go to 10buckplr.com, you are getting high quality PLR.

Most of these extra steps I mentioned aren't strictly necessary, but they are worth doing. They will add to your overall profits.

Show your faith by putting your name to the product that you have created from the PLR. This is excellent for personal branding and building up your own reputation.

From small acorns, the largest and mightiest oak trees grow.

And from small inconsequential PLR products, you can grow a massive and valuable business.

By following this advice, and taking action with PLR, you'll have an instant high quality product in almost no time. Then you really will be successfully writing with other people's content.

I wish you the very best.

Thom Lancaster
10BuckPLR.com